THE Wild LIFE OF Cows

A RUBES® CARTOON BOOK   BY LEIGH RUBIN

BOWTIE PRESS

IRVINE, CALIFORNIA

For Teresa, whose laughter is my inspiration.

Nick Clemente, Special Consultant
Karla Austin, Project Manager
Ruth Strother, Editor-at-Large
Michelle Martinez, Editor
Michael Vincent Capozzi, Designer

The author would like to gratefully acknowledge Paull for his twisted contributions.

Library of Congress Control Number: 2003102985

BowTie™ Press
A Division of BowTie Inc.
3 Burroughs
Irvine, California 92618
949-855-8822

Printed and Bound in Singapore
10 9 8 7 6 5 4 3 2 1

Foreword

What would toast be without butter? A baked potato without sour cream? A hot fudge sundae without whipped cream? Or—gasp!—a latté without milk?!
Pretty hard to imagine, eh?

Well, it's about time we acknowledge those four-legged beasts who have given us so much and asked for so little in return. The next time you find yourself craving a mouth-watering milk chocolate bar; ordering a milkshake with your fries; having some cheese on your burger; or indulging in a double scoop of French vanilla, Rocky Road, or Chocolate Chip Cookie Dough ice cream, take a moment and give thanks to cows everywhere. For without them life as we know it would be udderly unthinkable.

Leigh Rubin

"Yes, dear, you can go outside and play, but watch where you step. Your father's been fertilizing again."

Calves can be so cruel.

Squirt gun fights on the dairy farm.

"Oh, dear. I think Harriet may have spent a bit too much time in the tanning booth."

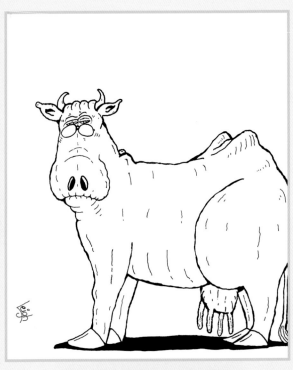

Where sour cream comes from

Double burgers prior to processing.

"Really, Al, if you must make methane, please go into another room."

"Well, that does it—no more using our heads!"

Millie suffered the embarrassment
of bovine incontinence.

"Mmmm… there's nothing like the smell of us cookin' over an open fire!"

"What a drag! We've been unsuccessfully trying to thumb a ride all day. Then again, I suppose it would help if we had thumbs."

"Body piercing! Tattoos! Boy, those humans certainly are a strange breed!"

"Hey, Mom! Clyde's drinking milk out of the container!"

"Poor Edna, she was so young (sigh). You just never know when your expiration date will be up."

"Howdy, fellas! I'm back! Say, I don't suppose either of you noticed a touch of irony in my tragic little mishap?"

The dedication it takes to bring half-and-half to your local restaurant.

"For goodness sake, Harriet—were you raised in a barn?!"

The mother goose café—post humpty

"What nerve! Here they come again! What do you suppose the neighbors did for milk before we moved in?!"

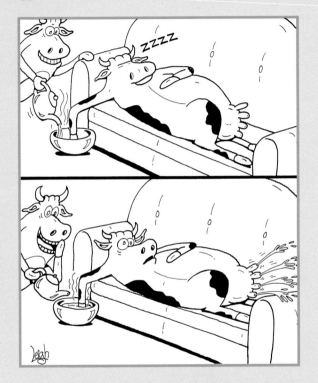

"Here comes Danny. If I were you I wouldn't be so eager to help him out with his homework again."

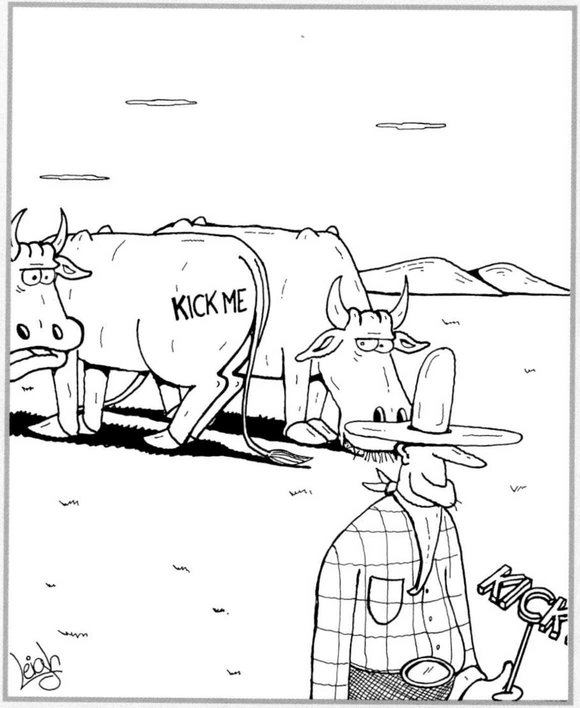
KICK ME
KICK

"I'm not at all sure that I appreciate his particular brand of humor."

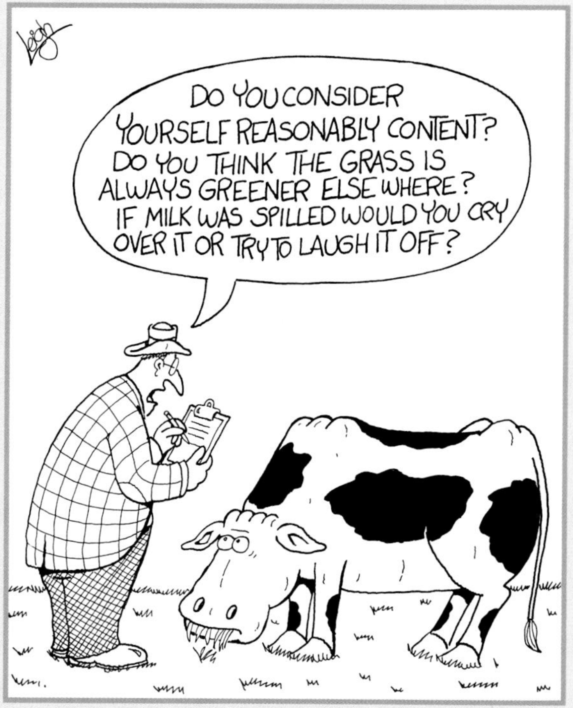
DO YOU CONSIDER YOURSELF REASONABLY CONTENT? DO YOU THINK THE GRASS IS ALWAYS GREENER ELSE WHERE? IF MILK WAS SPILLED WOULD YOU CRY OVER IT OR TRY TO LAUGH IT OFF?

Polled heifers

"And if you can't wait until morning, use this."

Perhaps Edna should have been more specific when placing her personal ad seeking, "a big strong vegetarian animal lover."

Unfortunately the new world record holder for the high jump was burned to a crisp upon reentering the Earth's atmosphere.

After three days of the same unimaginative excuse, the boss began to suspect his employee was full of it—figuratively speaking.

Not content with what nature had provided her, Maude seriously considered udder implants.

"You may be right, Martha—maybe they are getting a bit too domesticated."

"Yes, I'm well aware that my nose is pierced,
but those are different!"

On the Half-and-Half Dairy Farm

"You take the one on the left. I'm allergic to dairy."

Where nonfat milk comes from

"Instead of a regular hamburger, may I recommend our new chicken supreme sandwich? It's healthier for you—and for me too."

It was a lovely centerpiece, much too lovely
for Maude to resist.

"As president of the dairy council, it is my pleas-
ure to present you with this Veterinarian of the
Year Award for your unselfish commitment and
dedication to helping udders."

Nothing matched the death-defying thrill of the herd firewalker.

"What's the problem?! Didn't you tell me to pick up some milk on the way home?!"

Frequently, the cows engaged in the time-honored practice of comparing udder size.

"And that's your Uncle Norm at the family barbecue—he's the one in between the two buns."

As popular as it was, Maude quickly decided against wallpapering in a Southwestern motif.

"Hey, fellas, get ready to score with some hot babes. I just overheard the ranch foreman say that he's takin' us to a meat market tonight!"

"That's it! If the two of you can't get along, I'm going to confine the two of you to your veal pens!"

Just one look at his mother's meat thermometer and Clyde miraculously felt well enough to go to school.

The dawn of latté

If the cow jumped over the moon today.

A self-fulling prophecy

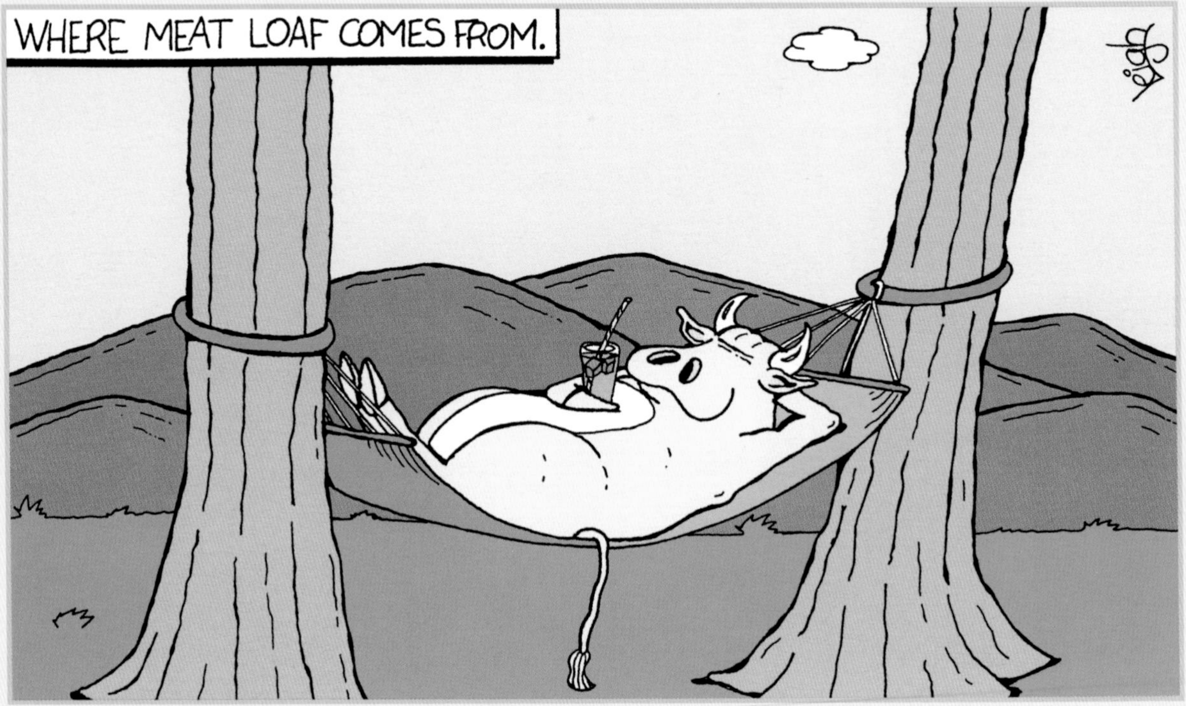
WHERE MEAT LOAF COMES FROM.

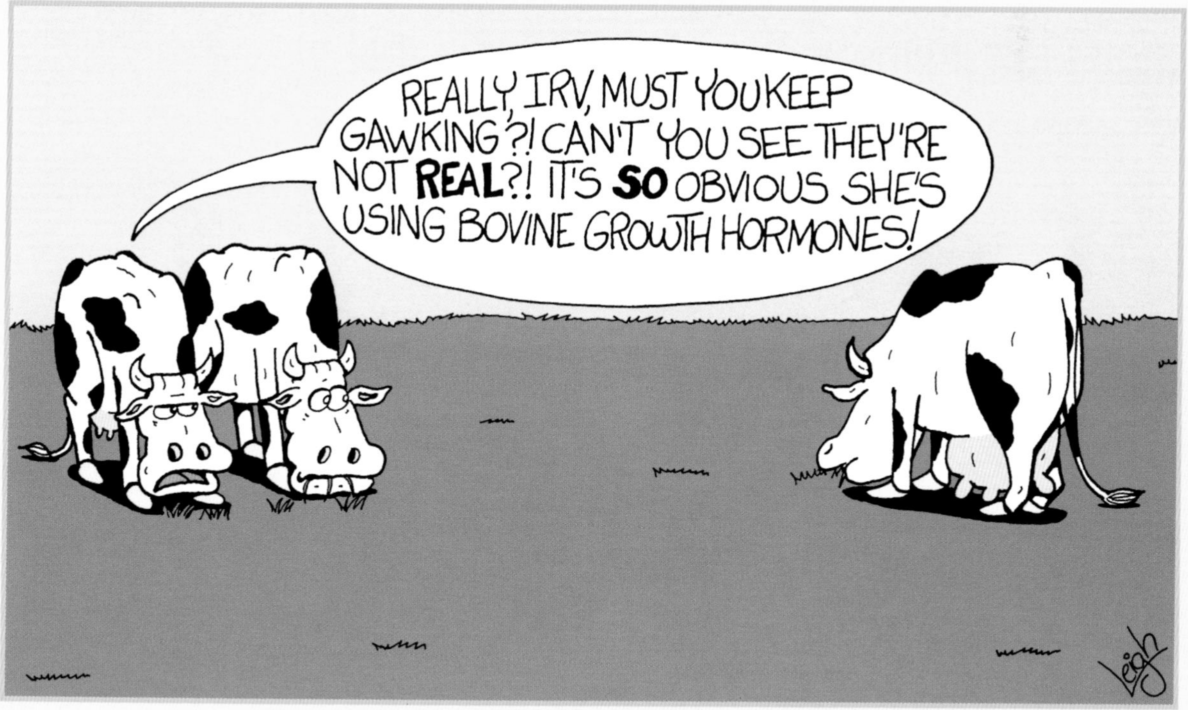
REALLY, IRV, MUST YOU KEEP GAWKING?! CAN'T YOU SEE THEY'RE NOT **REAL**?! IT'S **SO** OBVIOUS SHE'S USING BOVINE GROWTH HORMONES!
Leigh

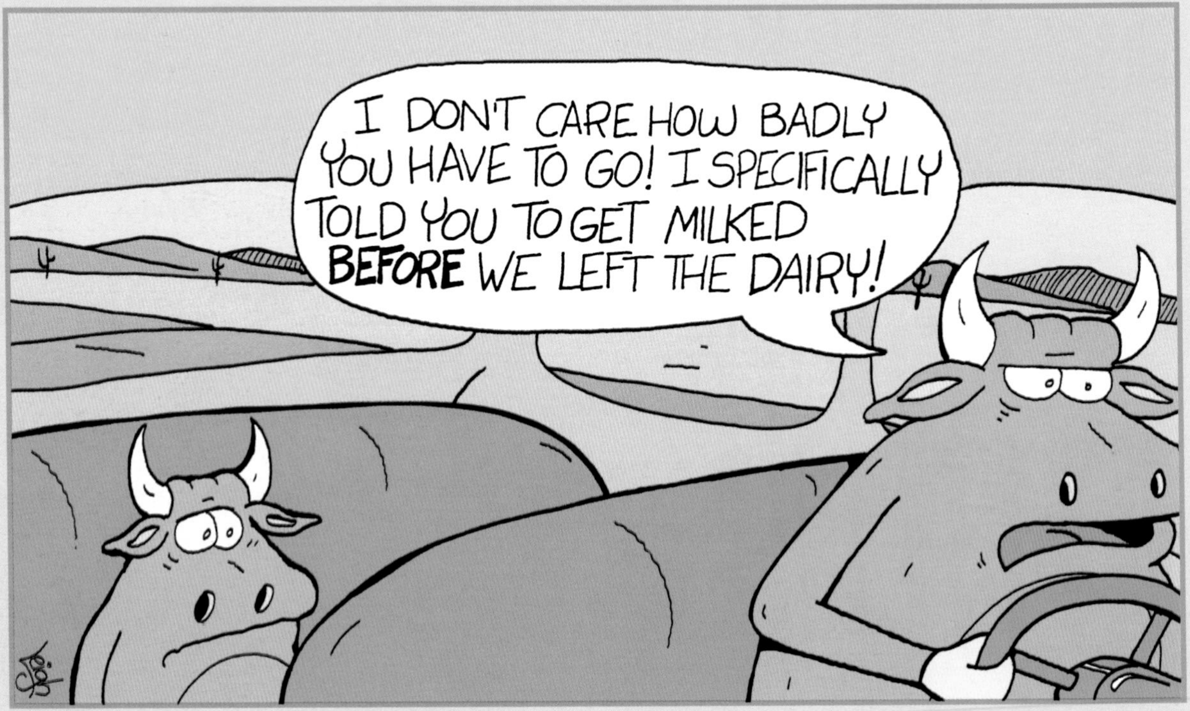
I DON'T CARE HOW BADLY YOU HAVE TO GO! I SPECIFICALLY TOLD YOU TO GET MILKED **BEFORE** WE LEFT THE DAIRY!

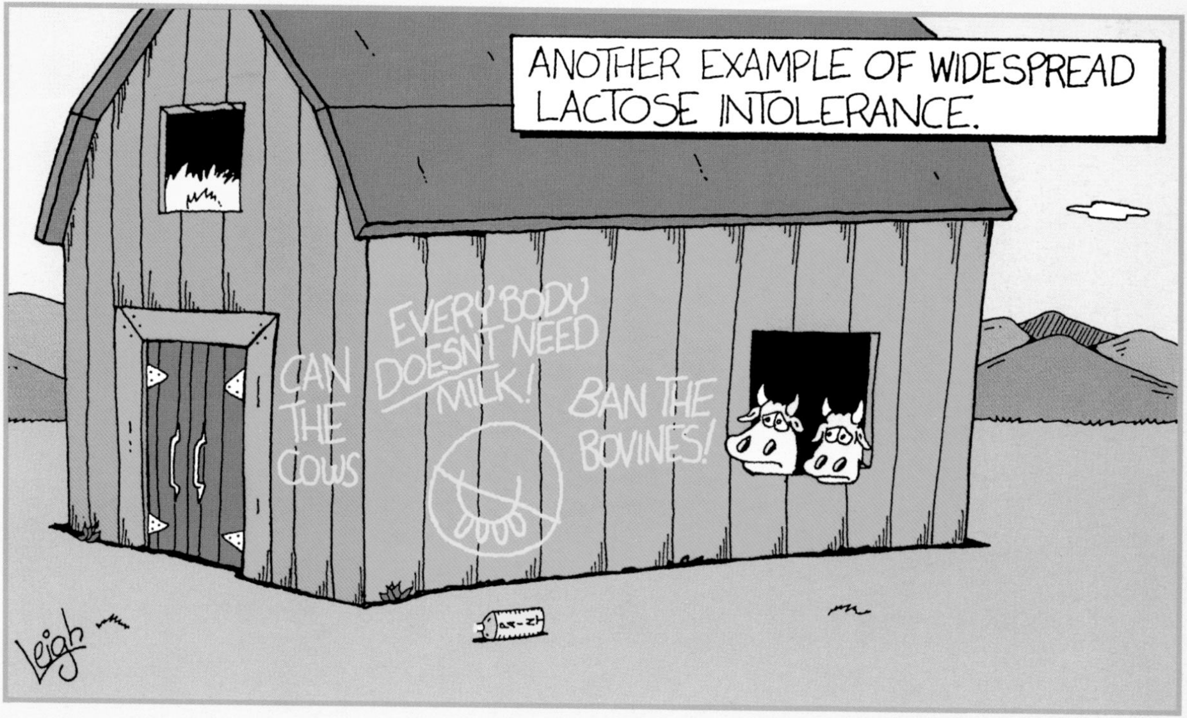
ANOTHER EXAMPLE OF WIDESPREAD LACTOSE INTOLERANCE.
CAN THE COWS
EVERYBODY DOESN'T NEED MILK!
BAN THE BOVINES!
Leigh

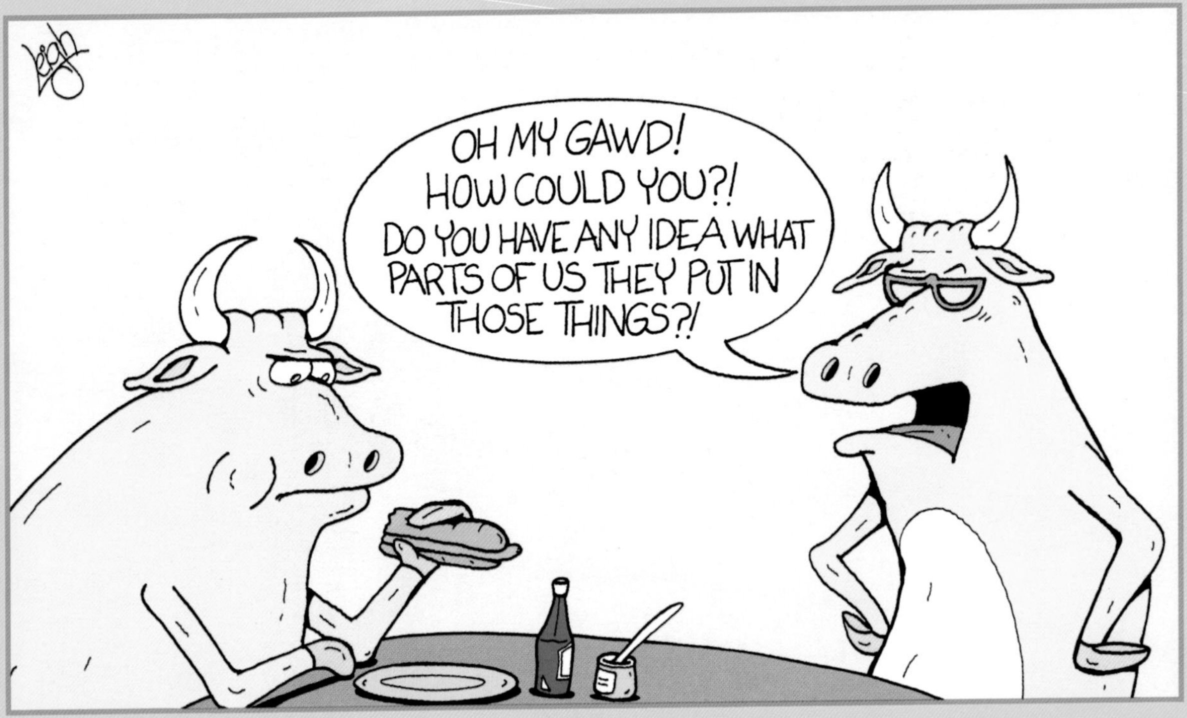
OH MY GAWD!
HOW COULD YOU?!
DO YOU HAVE ANY IDEA WHAT
PARTS OF US THEY PUT IN
THOSE THINGS?!

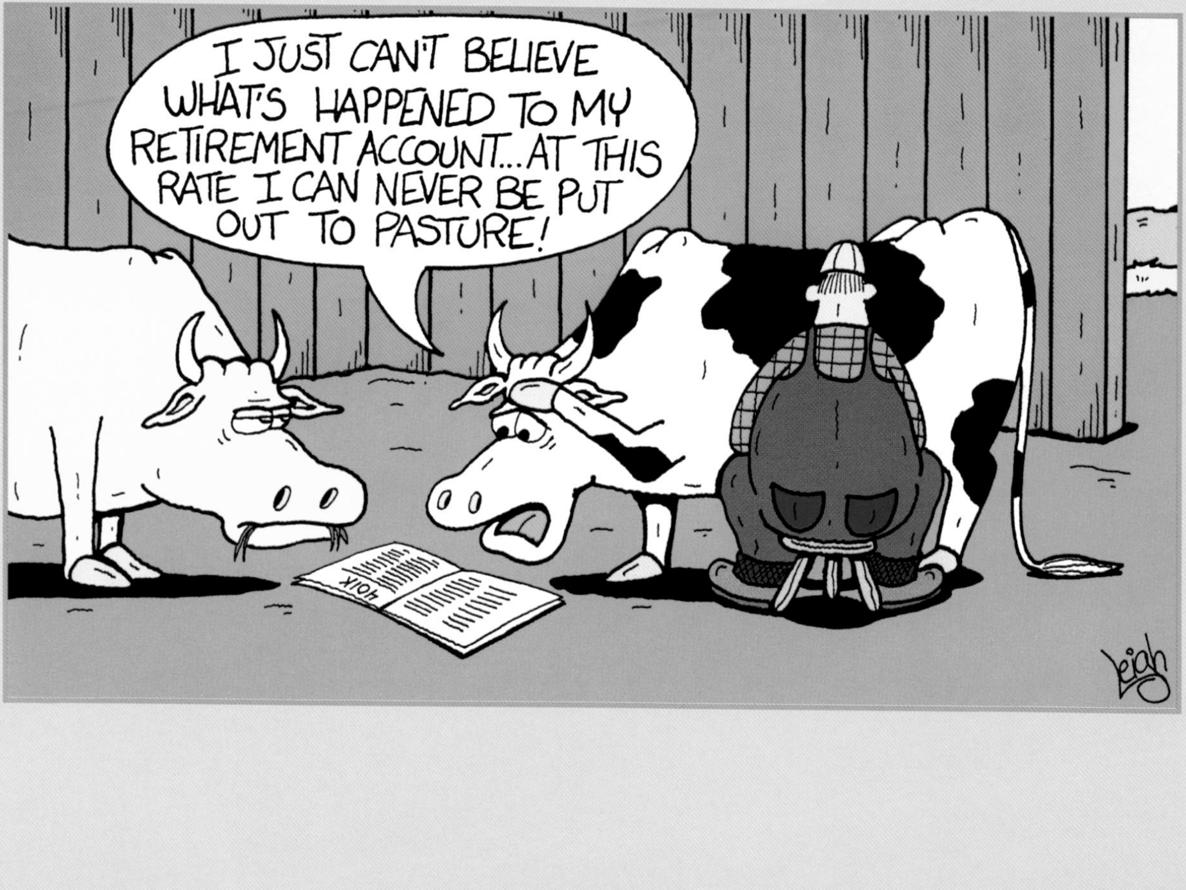
I JUST CAN'T BELIEVE WHAT'S HAPPENED TO MY RETIREMENT ACCOUNT...AT THIS RATE I CAN NEVER BE PUT OUT TO PASTURE!
401K
Leigh

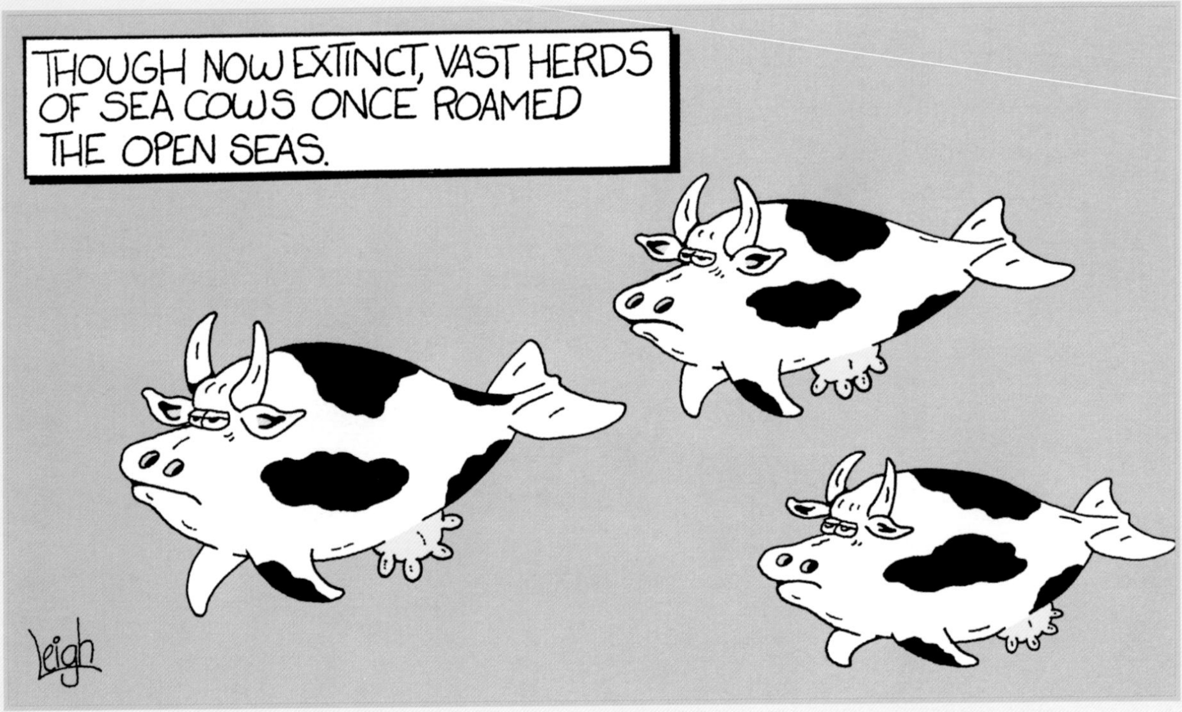
THOUGH NOW EXTINCT, VAST HERDS OF SEA COWS ONCE ROAMED THE OPEN SEAS.
Leigh

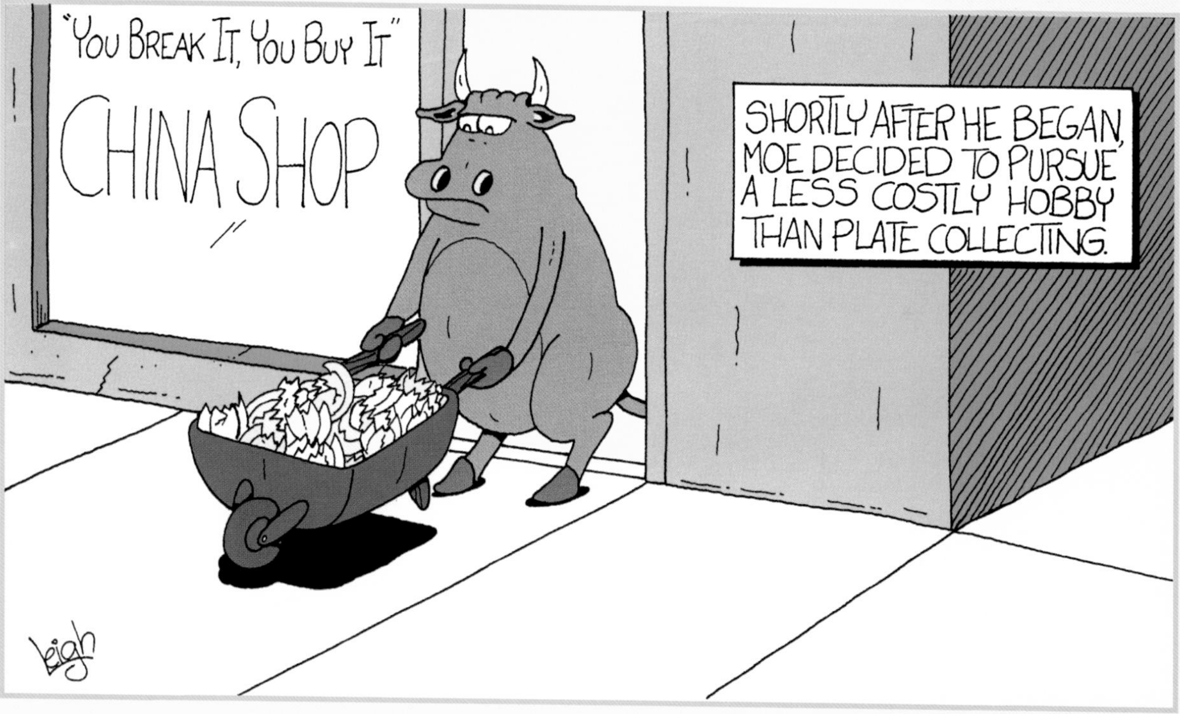
"YOU BREAK IT, YOU BUY IT"
CHINA SHOP
SHORTLY AFTER HE BEGAN, MOE DECIDED TO PURSUE A LESS COSTLY HOBBY THAN PLATE COLLECTING.
leigh

Bovine bunk beds

"I'm tired of the singles scene—men leering at me as if I were a piece of meat."

"Here you go—it's my famous liver and onions."

hamburger helper

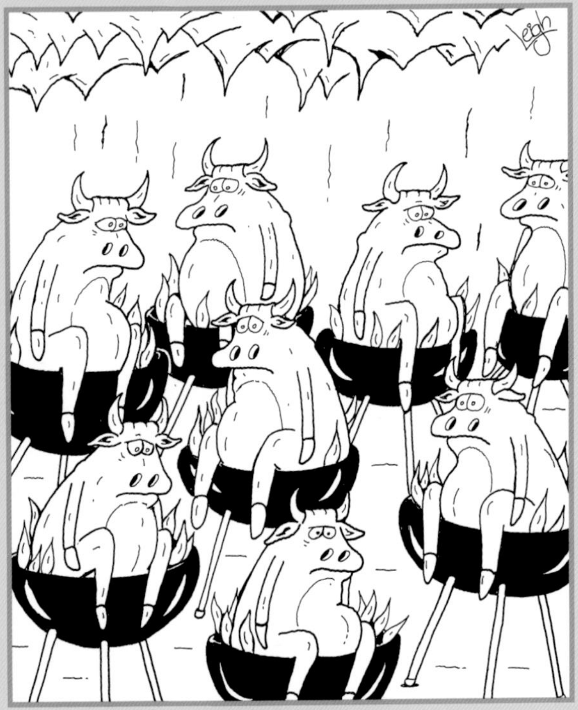
leigh

Cow hell

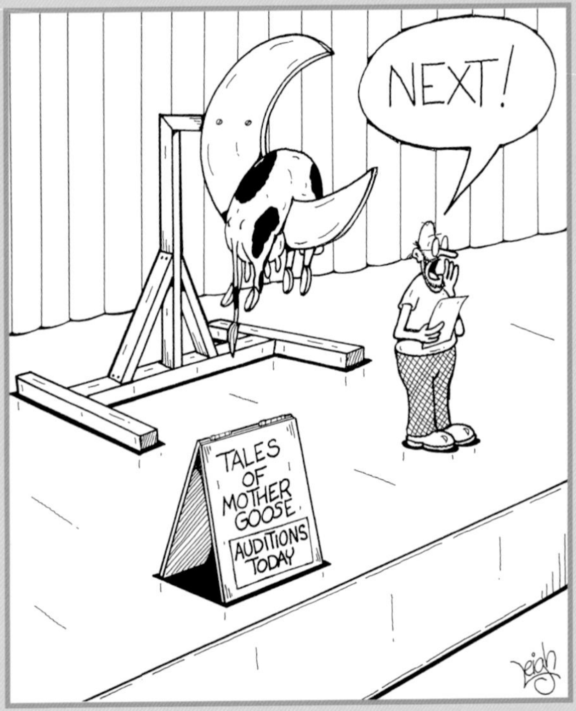
NEXT!
TALES OF MOTHER GOOSE
AUDITIONS TODAY
leigh

How bovine parents prevent stray calves.

Speculation as to whether or not Maude had her udders "done" became somewhat of a herd pastime.

42

Origins of overgrazing

"Well, I'm not surprised you flunked handwriting. For cryin' out loud—you can't even hold a pen!"

Even when practiced discreetly, raised eyebrows and disapproving glances still meet with those who dare to udder-feed in public.

On the Lean Beef Ranch

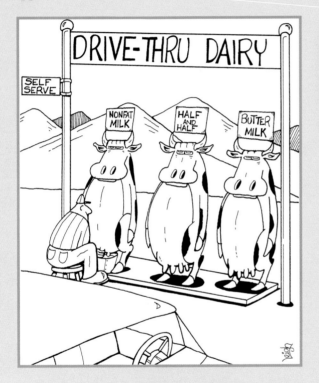

"There's no point losing sleep worrying about the bills—we'll just auction off the kids."

According to the latest study, the key to maintaining good health is to get plenty of exercise, eat lots of grains, and avoid red meat eaters.

"Goodness, Herb, you can't serve Chablis to our guest. You know perfectly well white wine doesn't go with beef!"

"Aha! So you've been in my closet again!"

"And according to the ranch veterinarian, the deceased died of an unusual condition rarely found in beef known as 'natural causes.' "

"I really hate accepting handouts, but just how am I supposed to stretch myself to feed a large family on a tight budget without a little hamburger helper?"

"You don't want to get on that guy's bad side—he has a lot of pull around here."

As soon as his parents found out, Clyde could almost certainly expect to have his rump severely tenderized.

Many dairy employees refused to submit to mandatory drug testing for illegal hormone abuse, claiming it violated their animal rights.

"Well, the good news is fewer people are eating beef—the bad news is more of us will be out of work."

Bovine "family values"

If cows had agents

"It's all over, fellas—ain't no way we can compete with a mechanical bull."

"It's just awful—more senseless slaughtering!
I tell you it's getting so you're not even safe in
your own barn!"

"This is disgraceful! Your grandfather was Grade A beef. I was Grade A beef. I just want to know why you didn't make the cut?!"

"Some may see this milk cartoon as half empty, while others may see it as half full. But I simply see it as half-and-half."

"Never take life for granted son. It could be round up today and ground up tomorrow."

**The most frustrating problem faced
by herbivore parents.**

**Under constant threat of cattle rustlers, ranch
security was beefed up.**

From the looks of things, Maude was about to be milked for everything she had.

"So, do you come to this barn often?"

"That was my favorite drum—you can either pay to have it fixed, or I can take it out of your hide."

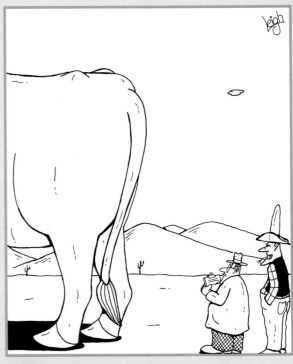

Despite the rancher's claim that no growth hormones were used on his livestock, the U.S.D.A. inspector had strong reason to believe otherwise.

The sexual harassment suit that sent shock waves through the dairy industry.

Dairy cows 5,000,000 B.C.

The dark secret behind chicken-fried steak.

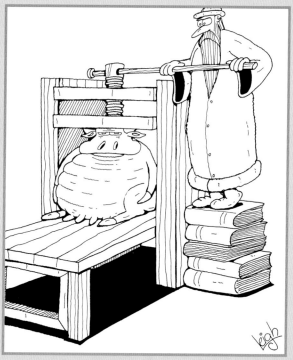

In addition to movable type, the famous German inventor was the first to devise a press specifically for making ground-beef patties, which he planned to market as Gutenbergers.

The horrible truth behind whipped cream.

"Study this chart, my young devotee, so that you may get to know your inner self."

"These guys are pounding each other into hamburger, chief. You'd better hurry up and send the patty wagon."

I'm going to have to ask you to leave, sir. We don't serve meat here.

**The special breed raised exclusively
for happy meals.**

Leigh Rubin has been creating RUBES® cartoons for eighteen years. They now appear in hundreds of newspapers worldwide and grace millions of greeting cards, mugs, T-shirts, and dog bowls. Leigh is the author of ten books including *The Wild Life of Dogs*, *The Wild Life of Pets*, *The Wild Life of Farm Animals*, *Rubes Bible Cartoons*, and the award-winning *Rubes-Then and Now*. Leigh is married and has three sons.

BowTie™ Press is a division of BowTie Inc., which is the world's largest publisher of pet magazines. For further information on your favorite pets, look for *Dog Fancy*, *Dogs USA*, *Cat Fancy*, *Cats USA*, *Horse Illustrated*, *Bird Talk*, *Reptiles*, *Aquarium Fish*, *Rabbits*, *Ferrets USA*, and many more.